Can Your Faith Fail?

by
Charles Capps

HARRISON HOUSE
Tulsa, Oklahoma

15th Printing
Over 125,000 in Print

Can Your Faith Fail?
ISBN 0-89274-105-8
Copyright © 1978 by Charles Capps
Box 69
England, Arkansas 72046

Published by Harrison House, Inc.
P. O. Box 35035
Tulsa, Oklahoma 74153

CAN YOUR FAITH FAIL?

FAITH IS A LAW

Faith is of God. God is a faith God. Without faith it is impossible to please Him. Faith is a law (Romans 3:28; 8:7). God's laws work. They were designed to work—not fail. Whether others believe or don't believe will not stop God's laws from working.

". . . what if some did not believe? shall their unbelief make the faith of God without effect? God forbid: yea, let God be true, but every man a liar; as it is written, That thou mightest be justified in thy sayings, and mightest overcome when thou art judged" (Romans 3:3,4).

FAITH COMES FROM A SUPERNATURAL SEED

THE FAITH OF GOD DOES NOT FAIL. Faith comes by the Word of God (Romans 10:17).

The Word of God is incorruptible seed. A natural seed will sometimes fail: God's

Word never fails. Many times people fail to apply the Word of God.

You can cause faith to fail to produce. Let's say it this way: **True faith is a supernatural seed; it won't fail, but you can cause a failure** in spite of the seed. Your action or reaction can stop the productivity of the seed. The seed (faith) does not always determine the outcome. "And the Lord said, If ye had faith as a grain of mustard seed, ye might say to this sycamine tree, Be thou plucked up by the root, and be thou planted in the sea; and it shall obey you" (Luke 17:6). "We having the same spirit of faith, according as it is written, I believed, and therefore have I spoken; we also believe, and therefore speak" (2 Corinthians 4:13).

"SATAN HATH DEMANDED TO HAVE YOU . . . ."

Although you have faith, evidently it is possible for it to fail to produce the desired results. We see this possibility of failure in Luke 22:31,32: "And the Lord said, Simon,

4

Simon, behold satan hath desired to have you, that he may sift you as wheat: But I have prayed for thee, that thy faith fail not . . . ."

Notice, it does NOT say, "God hath desired to sift you," but "satan hath desired to sift you." The Greek word translated desired means **demanded.** Satan had demanded to have Peter that he might sift him as wheat. So often people think God is doing the testing and trying, so they just bow down to it, try to be humble, and bear the trial. They suffer whatever comes their way because they believe it is God perfecting them. Many will quote a verse of Scripture out of context to prove it is God doing it.

For example, people say, "You know the Bible says, 'All things work together for good.'"

Yes, Paul did say that in Romans 8:28, but let us keep it in the context of what Paul was teaching. "Likewise the Spirit also helpeth our infirmities: for we know not

5

what we should pray for as we ought: but the Spirit itself maketh intercession for us with groanings which cannot be uttered. And he that searcheth the hearts knoweth what is the mind of the Spirit, because he maketh intercession for the saints according to the will of God. **And we know** that all things work together for good to them that love God, to them who are the called according to his purpose" (Romans 8:26-28). Paul said after you have prayed in the spirit, **then** you know that **all things** you prayed about by interceding in the spirit will work together for good.

THE GREATEST ENEMY OF FAITH

The greatest enemy of faith, the most subtle and the most devastating, is **the lack of knowledge of the Word of God.** To believe the devil's lie that, "It is God that is putting you through trials and tests:" will neutralize your faith. Through religious tradition satan has blinded the minds of Christians to what the Word says. Jesus said, *"SATAN HATH DESIRED TO . . . SIFT YOU."*

James 1:2 says, ". . . count it all joy when ye fall into divers temptations." Notice, he said, "when you fall into temptations," not when you walk into them with your eyes open. Some folks have walked into them with their eyes wide open! This verse is often misquoted as, "The trying of your faith perfects it." But the Word says, "The trying of your faith works patience."

Patience is a spiritual force that will support your faith like a pier under a bridge. Satan tries that which you call "faith" to see if it is true faith, or if it is mental assent. **The force of patience will undergird your faith and cause you to be constant** — holding the same confession through the trial satan brought.

SATAN IS OUT TO DESTROY YOUR FAITH

Peter said, ". . . think it not strange concerning the fiery trial which is to try you, as though some strange thing happened unto you: But rejoice, inasmuch as ye are partakers of Christ's sufferings

. . . " (1 Peter 4:12,13). No, it's not strange that these things happen. Satan is not out to perfect your faith. If the trying of your faith perfected it, we would all have it made. Our faith would be perfect. I don't know anyone who hasn't had plenty of trials or tests!

I'll admit that if you win out with your faith, you will be stronger. **If you'll put your faith into action through the Word, you will come out with a determination to not let satan win another battle.** But that is not what satan designed it to do. He designed the trial to put you under, not over.

Trials are a design of satan. If you believe that God sends trials, that is a devastating blow to your faith. If God is doing it, certainly you don't want to resist God. For instance, in the area of sickness, if it's God's will for you to be sick, why go to a doctor and try to get out of God's will?

It is God's will that you be well. "Beloved, I wish above all things that thou mayest prosper and be in health, even as

8

thy soul prospereth" (3 John 2). God wants you healed, and He will go any way you choose: through doctors, through the Word, or both. But, if you fall for satan's lie, *your faith is in neutral.* You cannot use your faith to get rid of something you believe God gave you.

Satan is not the finisher of your faith, and if trials and tests perfected faith, satan would be the finisher of it. Hebrews 12:2 declares that *Jesus is the author and finisher of your faith.*

GOD IS NOT THE TEMPTER

Let me call your attention to something Jesus said when He was teaching His disciples principles of prayer. "After this manner therefore pray ye: Our Father which art in heaven, Hallowed be thy name. Thy kingdom come. Thy will be done in earth as it is in heaven" (Matthew 6:9,10). Just stop and ask yourself this question: Is it God's will that we be tested and tried in heaven? The answer is obvious. There will be no tests or trials there. Then, that must be God's will for the earth.

In Matthew 26:41, Jesus said to His disciples, "Watch and pray, that ye enter not into temptation . . . ." Evidently you can avoid temptations, tests, and trials by watching and praying. Most of the time we get into trials and temptations by not doing what Jesus said to do to avoid them.

The word *temptation* in James 1:2, ". . . count it all joy when ye fall into divers *temptations*," and in verse 13, "Let no man say when he is *tempted* I am *tempted* of God . . . ." is the same word translated *trial* and *test* in other parts of the New Testament. Let's paraphrase it: "Let no man say that it is God doing the tempting and trying: for God cannot be tempted with evil, neither tempteth He any man."

"Do not err, my beloved brethren." Or as we would say, do not be misled. "Every good gift and every perfect gift is from above, and cometh down from the Father of lights, with whom is no variableness, neither shadow of turning" (James 1:16,17).

The word *shadow* here speaks of less light or darkness. There is never any gradual turning from that which is good and perfect. God is not guilty of using evil or darkness to perfect you.

TWO FORCES AT WORK

The Father is the giver of all good. In John 10:10, Jesus said, "The thief cometh not, but for to steal, and to kill, and to destroy: I am come that they might have life . . ." Thank God that He came to bring life, not trials. There are two opposing forces: the force of evil and the force of righteousness. The force of evil steals, kills and destroys. If you let him, satan will steal your faith, kill your testimony, and destroy your health. He'll do anything to destroy you. The force of righteousness is from God who gave Jesus to provide life more abundantly. This force works for you; the other works against you. The force working against you is in no way working for you. You can write that down. That opposing force is not working a good in you. It was designed to destroy your faith and to keep you from pleasing God. That is the design of satan.

Jesus said you could avoid some of those temptations by watching and praying: "And lead us not into temptation," or "Lead us not into any way that we would be tempted, tested, or tried." If testing and trials would perfect their faith, I wonder why Jesus didn't know it? He is the author of our faith.

Now, if Jesus authored your faith, don't you know that He does not have to try it to see if it will work? General Motors wouldn't be so foolish to build a car, sell it to someone, and then try it out to see if it would run. When their trademark goes on it, they know that it will work. It has already been proven. Jesus authored your faith. It is His faith. It has already been tried and proven; it works. He never did make any unworthy workmanship. We are His workmanship, He authored us and our faith: (Ephesians 2:10; Hebrews 12:2).

LACK OF WORD EQUALS
LACK OF FAITH

How does faith come? Faith comes by hearing the Word of God (Romans 10:17). A lack of faith is caused from a lack of the Word. Christians have a lack of faith because the Word does not abide in them, **If God's Word is in you, faith is there.** If satan comes along with his smoke screen and says, "This is God trying and testing you," most people will just melt and have a pity party. They cry, "Why me, Lord?"

Don't allow satan to bring every bad thing that comes down the road to you. "Neither give place to the devil" (Ephesians 4:27). It is not God perfecting you. Many books have been written out of self-pity and defeat. Many people fall under the attack of satan, and say, "It must be God perfecting me." That is a cop-out. It is easier to blame God than to admit that we failed to act on the Word. This kind of thinking is a devastating blow to anyone's faith. It will stop your faith from working.

Your faith will fail to produce when you fall for satan's lies. It was not the law of faith that failed— you failed to apply the law because of lack of knowledge.

Jesus said for us to pray that we would not be led in any way that we would be tempted, tested, or tried. Sure, trials and tests are going to come. Peter said, "Think it not strange when they do come, but to rejoice inasmuch as you are partakers of Christ's sufferings." What are the sufferings of Christ that Peter was talking about? *Persecutions.* The Bible says that those who live godly will suffer persecutions. Now —*don't go believing for persecution.* Actually, they caused most of it because of the foolish things they did. They thought they were suffering for Jesus, but they suffered for a lack of knowledge.

Let's look at another Scripture that some believe says that we are to accept everything that comes our way. I can see where people who have been taught that way would believe that it is so. We read in 1 Peter 4:1, "Forasmuch then as Christ hath suffered for us in the flesh, arm yourselves likewise with the same mind . . . ." Let me say it like most people read it: "Christ suffered for us in the flesh, so we must suffer sickness and disease in our flesh for Jesus. We must suffer the tests and trials of life for Jesus." That's not what Peter said; nothing could be farther from the truth. Peter said, "Forasmuch then as Christ hath suffered for us in the flesh, arm yourselves likewise with the **same mind**." What is the same mind? *That Christ suffered for you* **in the flesh that you wouldn't be bound to suffering, but could be delivered from it.** Arm yourselves with the same mind: that Jesus did your suffering for you (Isaiah 53:5). Tell the enemy, "You can't put that junk on me. I won't have it, Jesus did my suffering. Jesus bore my sickness and diseases. You can't put that junk on me; that's illegal."

Galatians 3:13 says, "Christ **hath** redeemed us from the curse of the law, being made a curse for us . . . ." How was He made a curse for us? Isaiah 53:9

literally says that God made Him sick. The chastisement needful to obtain peace and well being for us was upon Him (Isaiah 53:5). The chastisement that Jesus suffered was different from that spoken of in the New Testament. Hebrews 12:6 ". . . whom the Lord loveth he chasteneth . . . ." That word *chasten* in the Greek means to teach, instruct, or child train. You train a child *with words*. You would say, "No, don't do that. Don't touch the stove." You wouldn't stick your child's hand to a stove, burn a blister on it and say, "Now, don't do that because I love you. I want to teach you something." They have prisons where they put people that do such things. Our civil laws forbid such things. Still, people want to accuse God of doing that to His children. This is an enemy of faith. You wouldn't want to come against something that was perfecting you. It is much easier to feel sorry for yourself.

WHAT YOU ALLOW, GOD WILL ALLOW

When you feel one of those pity parties coming on and want to feel sorry for yourself, you can mark it down: satan is on your case. If he can get you to feel sorry for yourself, your reaction usually is, "Oh, Lord, why did you allow this to happen to me?" That's a foolish question. God will allow anything you will allow. He'll let you rob a bank if you want to. God will allow you to go to hell if you want to. You are foolish if you do either one, but God will allow it. It's sure not His will, but He will allow you to do it.

The Bible says that Jesus came and died that all would be saved and none would be lost (John 3:16), but God will still let you go to hell if you want to. The decision is yours, not God's. This is where we have missed it. Somebody said, "God allowed it; so it must have been His will." Nothing could be further from the truth. That is a lie of satan. Adam and Eve sinned in the garden of Eden, but it wasn't God's will. It couldn't have been, because God told Adam not to do it. The decision was Adam's. God allows sin, but He is certainly not in favor of it. God allows sickness, but it is not His will.

Somebody says, "Yes, but if Christ redeemed us from the curse of sickness, then no one would ever be sick." Just stop and ask yourself these questions: Did He redeem us from sin? Yes. Is anyone sinning today? Yes. Then you can see how foolish it is to think that way. We are redeemed from the curse of the law, but you can still be sick. All you have to do to prove that is—do nothing, and you will be sick.

Many banks are robbed every month, but you wouldn't accuse the president of the United States of doing it or even allowing it. You wouldn't say, "It happened under his administration; so we're going to blame it all on him." That's the same as blaming God for things that happen to us. That is a cop-out. It is religious thinking. Sometimes things happen because we fail to watch and pray.

THE BLESSINGS AND CURSES OF THE LAW

Psalm 107:2 says, "Let the redeemed of the Lord say so, whom he hath redeemed from the hand of the enemy;" Christ has redeemed us from the curse of the law. In Deuteronomy 28, God told the children of Israel of the blessing and the curses of the law. He said, "If you'll hearken diligently unto the voice of the Lord thy God, you'll be blessed in the city, blessed in the field, blessed coming in, blessed going out . . . ." They would be blessed all over more than anywhere else. There wasn't any way they could go without being blessed. If they hearkened diligently to the voice—God's Word, the blessings of God would come upon them and overtake them. That meant that they couldn't run fast enough to get away from the blessings. In other words, God said, "If you get over there in disobedience to this commandment, all these blessings will become curses. You'll be cursed in the city, cursed in the field, cursed in the basket, cursed in the store. You'll have financial and physical defeat." In verse 60, God said all of the diseases that they were redeemed from would become a part of the curse, and He included any disease or plague not yet mentioned. These curses would come upon them if they got over there where the curses were.

The King James translation says, ". . . the Lord will make thy plagues wonderful . . . ." (Deuteronomy 28:59), and ". . . he will bring upon thee all the diseases . . . ." (Verse 60). If you read that and don't understand what happened, you will think that God was the cause of it. He was not the cause. Their disobedience was the cause. God told them what would happen if they walked in disobedience. The curses were already established. The children of Israel walked where God said not to walk, and the curses slapped them right in the face. Then God is accused of doing it. He didn't. He made every provision to keep them away from the curses. The children of Israel caused it in spite of all God did to keep them from the curses. God's Word was out.

Just because they were foolish enough to be disobedient doesn't mean God's Word would change. God cannot lie or change His Word. He will not alter that which has come out of His mouth. What really caused it to come to pass? Their disobedience activated the curse and God's Word was proven to be true. Then, because their disobedience received a just reward, many blame God for the curse.

Sometimes we get a distorted image of God from reading the Old Testament, especially in the Scripture where it says that God sent these things. The children of Israel cried and said, "We wish we had died in the wilderness." God told Moses to tell them, "As truly as I live . . . as ye have spoken in mine ears, so will I do to you" (Numbers 14:28). In other words, God said, "I'll do exactly what you say."

What did they say?

"And the people spake against God, and against Moses, Wherefore have ye brought us up out of Egypt to die in the wilderness? for there is no bread, neither is there any water; and our soul loatheth this light bread" (Numbers 21:5).

The King James Version of the Bible states that God sent fiery serpents among them. No: God didn't do it at all. It was their own words that caused the fiery serpents to come. God had already said, "I will do what you say." They said, "We are going to die." Fiery serpents came among them, bit them and they died like flies. Their own mouths set it in motion. GOD DID NOT DO IT. **Their words caused it to come to pass.** God told them it would happen exactly as "you say in my ear." Proverbs 18:21, tells us that life and death are in the power of the tongue. You can see that it is not God that is responsible for all these things.

Satan has tried to distort the image of God in the minds of His people. But those who seek the truth shall find it. God is not your problem: He is your answer.

Atheists and agnostics are the result of a distorted image of God. They say, "Surely there wouldn't be a God that would do that." They'd rather believe that there is no God than to believe the lies about God.

God's Word rules. When you break God's Word, He can't go back on His Word. It will come to pass.

WHAT ABOUT JOB?

Jesus said to Peter, ". . . satan hath desired to have you, that he may sift you as wheat." The Greek says, "Satan has **demanded** to have you . . . ." Let's look at another instance where this happened. Satan demanded to have Job.

It seems like everyone says, "Well, what about Job?" I was going through some trials one time; I sat up all night reading about Job, and wallowing in self-pity. I was so sure I was another Job, that I wanted to see how it all turned out. I was ready for that trial to be over. I guess at some time in life, everyone has said, "Oh Lord, I must be another Job." Job got healed and received twice as much as he had before!

Job 1:3 tells us, "His substance was also seven thousand sheep, and three thousand camels, and five hundred yoke of oxen, and five hundred she asses, and a very great household; so that this man was the greatest of all the men of the east."

23

"Now there was a day when the sons of God came to present themselves before the Lord, and satan came also among them. And the Lord said unto satan, Whence comest thou? Then satan answered the Lord, and said, From going to and fro in the earth, and from walking up and down in it. And the Lord said unto satan, Hast thou considered my servant Job, that there is none like him in the earth, a perfect and an upright man, one that feareth God, and escheweth evil? Then satan answered the Lord, and said, Doth Job fear God for nought? Hast not thou made an hedge about him, and about his house, and about all that he hath on every side? thou hast blessed the work of his hands and his substance is increased in the land" (Job 1:6-10).

This is the indictment satan brought against God: "You have put a hedge about Job, his house, and all that he has on every side. You blessed the work of his hand and his substance is increased in the land."

I can just see God standing there, smiling and saying, "Yes, I'm guilty: I did it." We know it takes faith to please God (Hebrews 11:6). Evidently Job, at one time had his faith working, but faith can fail to produce.

"But put forth thine hand now, and touch all that he hath, and he will curse thee to thy face. And the Lord said unto satan, Behold, all that he hath is in thy power; only upon himself put not forth thine hand . . ." (Verses 11,12). If you have a center column reference in your Bible, you will have a footnote for the word *power* that says, *"hand."* "All that he hath is in thy hand."

Some say, "God put Job in satan's hand." No, He didn't. God said Job was already there. How did he get there? We need to know because many of us have been in the hand of satan for the same reason. We have put ourselves in his hand. Job 1:4,5 says, "And his sons went and feasted in their houses, every one his day; and sent and called for their three sisters to eat and to drink with them. And it was so, when the days of their feasting were gone about, that

Job sent and sanctified them, and rose up early in the morning, and offered burnt offerings according to the number of them all: for Job said, It may be that my sons have sinned, and cursed God in their hearts. **Thus did Job continually.**"

The Word says that without faith it is impossible to please God (Hebrews 11:6). In the same chapter, verse 4 says, "By faith Abel offered unto God a more excellent sacrifice than Cain . . . ." God received Abel's sacrifice because it was offered in faith. Faith was one thing that made it stand out. In those days you were supposed to believe in your sacrifices. The Bible says that Job offered his sacrifices continually. He got out of faith and into fear. Evidently, he listened to the voice of the enemy.

When things began to happen to him they happened quickly. In verse 16, it says, "While he was yet speaking, there came also another, and said, The fire of God is fallen from heaven, and hath burned up the sheep . . . ." There is a footnote for the words *fire of God*. The Hebrew says, "a great fire." Another translation says, "lightning." Some say that God did it. No, God didn't do it. God did not create lightning to kill cattle. God's purpose was for good. He doesn't create the storms and the tornadoes to destroy. That is a perversion of nature. It came about after sin entered the earth. Satan perverted that which God created. The atmosphere was to bring rain upon the earth for good, but satan perverted it and used it for destruction. We do find in the Old Testament where God used nature to bring judgment, but we have to realize that we are not living under the Old Covenant today. We are under the dispensation of grace.

Let's look at Job 1:21 to gain greater insight into what happened to Job. Job said, ". . . Naked came I out of my mother's womb, and naked shall I return thither: the Lord gave, and the Lord hath taken away; blessed be the name of the Lord." If you have ever been to a funeral, you have most likely heard that quoted. It is true

27

that Job did say it, but it is not a true statement. It is a lie. Did you know there are lies recorded in the Bible? Now stay with me! Don't throw this book away. It will turn out all right. Ananias and Sapphira told Peter they had sold their land for so much, but they hadn't. That was a lie and it is recorded in the Bible. Someone might say, "But the Bible says, 'All Scripture is inspired of God.' "

It doesn't say that at all. It says in 2 Timothy 3:16, "All scripture is **given by inspiration** of God, and is profitable for doctrine, for reproof, for correction, for instruction in righteousness." Job 1:21 needs to be used for reproof. Job sure was not under the anointing when he made that statement. He could not read chapter 1 of the book of Job. So he had an excuse for saying what he did. But it was not God that took it away; God is the one who gave it. It was satan that took away everything Job had, and it was God who gave him twice as much as he had before.

"In all this Job sinned not, nor charged

God foolishly" (Verse 22). Job didn't charge God foolishly; he really believed what he was saying. He was convinced it was God that took it away. He was trying to be humble by saying in so many words, "The Lord took it away; who am I to fight against God?" His faith failed for lack of knowledge. It took nine months for him to get out from under this trial because it had neutralized his faith.

FAITH AND FEAR

In Job 3:25, he let the cat out of the bag: "For the thing which I greatly feared is come upon me, and that which I was afraid of is come unto me." Faith and fear are opposite forces. Fear is of the devil, and faith is of God. "Now faith is the substance of things hoped for, the evidence of things not seen" (Hebrews 11:1). Faith is the substance of things desired, and fear is the substance of things not desired. Job said the thing he greatly feared had come upon him. It always will. When fear comes in, faith goes out. God has not given us a spirit of fear, but of love, of power and of a sound mind. **Fear is faith in the devil.**

On almost every occasion when Jesus approached the disciples, He said, "Fear not." He told Jairus to fear not, when others said his daughter was already dead. Fear will destroy the operation of faith in the human spirit.

In Luke 21:26 Jesus said in the end time men's hearts would fail them for fear. Now, there is possibly a two-fold meaning to that; however, I have not found anywhere in the Bible where Jesus talked about the physical heart. I don't think that He was talking about the physical heart here, but about the inner man—the human spirit. The human spirit is designed to put you over in life. He was saying, "When the heart becomes paralyzed with fear, it won't work for you."

Job allowed fear to come in and it shut his inner man down, neutralized his faith and the thing that he greatly feared came upon him. Notice it says, "He greatly feared." He didn't just fear. He was highly developed in this fear. **When you become highly developed in either faith or fear, it will take less time for the manifestation to come.** That's the reason some of you say, "When I make a good confession it takes three months for it to come to pass, but just let me say one negative thing and it happens the very next day." You are more highly developed in the negative. You're releasing more fear than you are faith.

FORMULA FOR DEFEAT

Now, look in Job 3:26; "I was not in safety, neither had I rest, neither was I quiet; yet trouble came." Now isn't that amazing? He did everything that brings defeat and it worked. There is the formula for defeat. If you follow that formula you will be defeated. The Word will guarantee it. (Proverbs 3:12; 3:21-26.)

LEARN FROM JOB

Job did several things the Bible says not to do. This account was given by inspiration of God. It was put in the Bible so that it would be instruction to us, so we wouldn't follow the same pattern as Job. I thank God that He inspired the men who wrote the Bible to put these things in it, so that we can see where they missed it. It is profitable for instruction. All Scripture is profitable. It is a lot better to read that the way of the transgressor is hard than to go out and experience it. It has been said that experience is the best teacher. That is not always true. You can get a million dollars worth of experience for half price and it's still not a bargain.

Job said in verse 26, "I was not in safety, neither had I rest, neither was I quiet; yet trouble came." Satan even admitted that Job was in safety: "Hath not thou made a hedge about him . . . ." (Job 1:10). Yes sir, God had done it! He had put a hedge about his house and about all he had on every side, and He blessed the works of his hands.

There is no doubt that satan told Job he was going to lose it all, some day. In

Job 1:21, you see how Job reasoned with the enemy's help: (Paraphrased) "It's too good to be true. God has really prospered me, but I'll probably lose it all before I die." When he got into trouble that was the first thing that came out. You can't hide what is in your heart; it will get in your mouth every time (Matthew 12:34).

You may think that I am being a little hard on Job, but I'm just pointing out some things that are profitable to you. God inspired the men of God to tell it like it was so we could understand and learn from it.

Job *was* in safety, but he worried; he fretted; he complained; he had a bad case of the *"What if's?"*. Have you ever had those? "Well, we are trusting God, but *what if* it doesn't work?" If you get a bad case of the *"What if's?"* your faith will fail to produce.

It didn't take Job long to get some insight into what was happening. Job 6:23 says, ". . . Deliver me from the enemy's hand? . . . Redeem me from the hand of the mighty?" He had already figured out that he was in the enemy's hand. You will notice also that Job saw the devil as being "the mighty one."

"Teach me, and I will hold my tongue . . . ." (v.24a). He realized that his words had something to do with it. ". . . and cause me to understand wherein I have erred" (v. 24b). He wasn't as perfect as he thought he was. When God said he was perfect (Job 1:8), the Hebrew means *sincere*.

A man once told me that God allowed all this to happen to Job because he knew Job was perfect and could stand it. You know very well who authored that thinking: satan. The Bible tells us to be perfect as God is perfect. I don't believe that God wants you to attain maturity and lose all you have. He is a rewarder of those who diligently seek Him. He said, "He that abideth under the shadow of the almighty would be under the shadow of His wing." He said, "A thousand shall fall at thy side and ten thousand at thy right hand, but it shall not come nigh thee" (Psalm 91:7). Choose to believe God. He also said that, "The angel of the Lord encampeth around them that fear Him, and delivereth them" (Psalm 34:7).

Job said he wasn't in safety. You see how satan can come in with his smoke screen and blur our image of God. Just little things like getting you to worry; be over concerned. Worry is a sin as much as some of these other things that we would never think of doing. A certain person was worrying over a problem. Someone told him, "It is a sin to worry."

He replied, "God gave me sense enough to worry, and I'm going to worry." No, God gave us sense not to worry.

Job said, "Cause me to understand wherein I have erred." We need to frame that phrase and hang it on the wall. "Be careful for nothing; but in every thing by prayer and supplication with thanksgiving let your requests by made known unto God" (Philippians 4:6).

We are beginning to see that the story of Job is quite different than most religious teaching. In Job 40:4,5, Job said, "Behold, I am vile; what shall I answer thee? I will lay mine hand upon my mouth. Once I have spoken; but I will not answer: yea, twice; but I will proceed no further." To paraphrase it, he said, "I am going to have to get this mouth shut up until I can find out what to say. In Job 42:3, we find, "Who is he that hideth counsel without knowledge? **Therefore have I uttered that I understood not**; things too wonderful for me, which I knew not." And we find in verse 7, ". . . My wrath is kindled against thee, and against thy two friends: for ye have not spoken of me *the thing that is right*, as my servant Job *hath*." In other words, Job had his speech straightened out. ". . . and my servant Job shall pray for you: for him will I accept: lest I deal with you *after your folly*, in that ye have not spoken of me *the thing which is right*, like my servant Job" (v. 8).

It would be good for us to see an example of what Job's comforters were saying: "Remember, I pray thee, who ever perished, being innocent? or where were the righteous cut off? Even as I have seen, they that plow iniquity, and sow wickedness, reap the same. **By the blast of God they perish, and by the breath of his nostrils are they consumed**" (Job 4:7-9).

"And the Lord turned the captivity of Job . . ." (Job 42:10). If the Lord turned Job's captivity, who had him captive? It must have been satan. When Job prayed for his friends, the Lord also gave him twice as much as he had before. In my Bible I wrote by that verse, *"Who did it? God did it."* Most people, that I have heard, try to make God the one that took Job's possessions. God didn't do it: satan did.

Then they *come up* with this: "Yes, but God allowed it." *God will allow anything you will allow.* He will allow fear to come in. He'll allow satan to steal your peace of mind if you don't resist him with the Word. If you begin to worry and fret, saying you're not in safety, the same thing that happened to Job can happen to you.

Your faith *can fail to work* for lack of knowledge. *Faith won't work unless you work it.* You can't believe any further than you have knowledge.

I have a plaque on my wall that says, **"Fear knocked at the door, Faith answered and no one was there."** When fear comes in, faith goes out. When faith is inside, fear cannot penetrate. Fear will defeat you every time. Fear is a design of satan and God will allow anything that you will allow. God will allow a man to take his own life, or He will give him eternal life for the asking.

EXAMPLE OF PETER

Jesus said to Peter, ". . . I will give unto thee the keys of the kingdom . . ." Where is the kingdom? The kingdom of God is within you. The kingdom of God is in your heart. ". . . whatsoever thou shalt bind on earth shall be bound in heaven: and whatsoever thou shalt loose on earth shall be loosed in heaven" (Matthew 16:19). Job loosed these things through fear. God told satan, "He is already in your hands." God didn't put him in satan's hands. He was already there through fear.

Satan demanded to have Peter to sift him as wheat. Why did he demand to have Peter?

Well, for one thing, Peter was quick to get in strife. Galatians 5:6 says, ". . . faith . . . worketh by love." Jesus said, ". . . Satan hath desired to have you, that he may sift you as wheat: But I have prayed for thee, that thy faith fail not . . ." (Luke 22:31,32). When you get out of the love walk, your faith will fail to produce. That does not mean that faith doesn't work, but when you get out of the love walk your faith will shut down. When you get into strife, you open the door to satan, and you may end up like Peter, or Job. Then you will want to ask, "Why me, Lord, why me?"

Let me remind you that Peter was a forward fellow, always getting himself into trouble by what he said. Someone has suggested peppermint flavored shoes for those who are always getting their feet in their mouths. Well, Peter needed them if ever anyone did. Before the day of Pentecost, he was always talking before he put his head in gear. Something happened there in that upper room, and he was never the same after that day. Until Peter received the Holy Ghost, nothing he did ever worked out.

Someone asks, "What is the Holy Spirit baptism with tongues of fire good for?"

Just take a look at Peter's life and that should convince you. He was a failure, going some where to happen. He went fishing and fished on the wrong side of the boat. He tried to walk on the water but, fearing, he began to sink. He even ran a race to Jesus' tomb and lost. But—after he received the Holy Ghost you never find him in failure again. In Acts 9:37,38, when Dorcas died, they sent for Peter instead of the undertaker.

Before he was filled with the Holy Spirit, Peter was quick to get into strife to say the least. Jesus perceived that, and prayed for him. When you get into strife and out of the faith walk, satan can demand to sift or try you. God can't do anything about it; you are in satan's territory; already in his hands. "For where envying and strife is, there is confusion and every evil work" (James 3:16).

When they came to get Jesus, Peter pulled out his sword and cut an old boy's ear off. Now, I think that you realize, he was not trying to cut off his ear; the man ducked. Peter was aiming for his head. You can see that wasn't a love slap.

Jesus said, "I have prayed for you, Peter, that your faith fail not." God's faith cannot fail. God is love. To operate in the God kind of faith you must walk in the God kind of love. Peter was not walking in love.

UNFORGIVENESS BLOCKS FAITH

When Jesus was talking about the God kind of faith in Mark 11:25, He said, "And when ye stand praying, forgive . . . ." Unforgiveness will stop your faith from working.

41

If I were having trouble getting my prayers answered, that's the first place I would look. I would ask, "Am I holding a grudge, or am I in unforgiveness?"

A lady came to a certain meeting and as the minister was preaching from Mark 11:25, about forgiving, the Holy Spirit convicted her. She hadn't spoken to her brother in twenty years; so she went across the street to a phone and called him. She apologized, and said that it was all her fault. Their fellowship was restored. She then decided she would go in the prayer line to receive her healing. She realized that unforgiveness was the reason she had not received her healing in the past. That night before the prayer line formed, every symptom had left her body. She was totally healed.

Sometimes people will ask, "Why am I not healed? I've been doing all the right formulas."

There are *principles* involved. Are you walking in love? Are you in envy or strife with your husband, wife, or your neighbor? Your faith will fail to produce if you live in strife or unforgiveness. You have opened the door to satan. You have invited him in and he will show up every time. Tragedy after tragedy has come to Christian homes because of *unforgiveness*.

In Matthew 18, Jesus told of the man who wouldn't forgive, and was then turned over to the tormentor. He was given into the hands, or delivered up to the tormentor until he paid the debt. The debt he owed was *forgiveness*. Jesus said, "So likewise shall my heavenly Father do also unto you, if ye from your hearts forgive not every one his brother their tresspasses" (v. 35). God is certainly not the tormentor. Jesus said, "The Father will have to deliver you into satan's hands, because He has no other choice" (Author's translation). You can see the parallel with satan demanding to have Peter.

Many faith people are saying the right things and doing the right formulas, but inside them is unforgiveness and strife.

43

Some won't talk to their brother in Christ. Then they have a car wreck: the whole family is injured, and they wonder why God allowed it to happen. It was not God's will but they were in the enemy's hands. Don't misunderstand what I said. I did not say everyone who has a car wreck is in unforgiveness. There are other things that can cause it, of course. But one of the major causes of tragedy in Christian homes is strife and unforgiveness. **Strife and unforgiveness will stop faith from working, and loose satan against your home.** The sin of unforgiveness produces fear, and fear destroys faith.

I don't have space in this book to teach further on unforgiveness, but I will deal with it in another book.

STIR UP YOUR FAITH

Paul wrote to Timothy: "When I call to remembrance the unfeigned faith that is in thee, which dwelt first in thy grandmother Lois, and thy mother Eunice; and I am persuaded that is in thee also. Wherefore I put thee in remembrance that thou **stir up the gift of God, which is in thee by the putting on of my hands.** For God hath not given us the spirit of fear; but of power, and of love, and of a sound mind" (2 Timothy 1:5-7).

What gift is given predominately in the Bible by the laying on of hands?

The gift of the Holy Spirit. Paul told Timothy to stir that gift up. Paul went on to say, "Hold fast the form of sound words, which thou hast heard of me, in faith and love which is in Christ Jesus. That good thing which was committed unto thee keep by the Holy Ghost which dwelleth in thee" (vv 13,14).

What good thing is he talking about?

Unfeigned faith. It was in Timothy's grandmother and his mother, and Paul was persuaded that it was also in him.

How are we going to keep unfeigned faith?

45

We keep it by the Holy Ghost which dwelleth in us. Do you know what it means to pray in the Holy Ghost? It is praying in the spirit or in tongues. Paul said, ". . . I will pray with the spirit, and I will pray with the understanding also" (1 Corinthians 14:15). It is an act of your will. It is the greatest force available today to you, as a believer—praying in the Holy Ghost.

Jude said that by praying in the Holy Ghost you build up yourselves on your most holy faith. He is talking about faith you already have inside you. He didn't say that praying in the Holy Ghost would give you more faith. He is talking about faith you already have inside you. He didn't say that praying in the Holy Ghost would give you more faith. Faith comes by hearing the Word of God. Timothy had faith because his mother and grandmother had evidently taught him the Word of God. When you get the Word in you, you have faith. It may not be stirred up, and you may not be using it, just as Timothy wasn't using his.

Paul said in Galatians 5:6, that faith

works by love. John said, "There is no fear in love; but perfect love casteth out fear: because fear hath torment. He that feareth is not made perfect in love" (1 John 4:18). When you have faith working by love there is no fear, but when fear comes in, faith goes out. Perfect love is not there for perfect love casts out fear.

Praying in the Holy Ghost builds you up on your most holy faith. Now this is exactly what Paul told Timothy when he told him to keep that good thing which was in him by the Holy Ghost. *You can have faith that does not produce anything.* **Praying in the Holy Ghost will stir up your faith and make it available so it will produce.**

"For he that speaketh in an unknown tongue speaketh not unto men, but unto God: for no man understandeth him; howbeit in the spirit he speaketh mysteries (divine secrets) . . . He that speaketh in an unknown tongue edifieth himself . . . ." (1 Corinthians 14:2,4). The word *edify* comes from the same Greek word from which we

47

have derived our word *charge*. If you had a
battery that was down and you took it to
the service station and asked them to
charge your battery, they would edify it, or
build it up. When you pray in the Holy
Ghost, it charges the spiritual power charge
of the inner man. **Praying in the Holy
Ghost stirs up the gifts of God which are in
you.** It stirs up the Word of God and makes
it available for use.

"But ye, beloved, building up yourselves on your most holy faith, praying in
the Holy Ghost. **Keep yourselves in the
love of God**, looking for the mercy of our
Lord Jesus Christ unto eternal life"
(Jude 20,21).

What did he say praying in the Holy
Ghost would do?

**Praying in the Holy Ghost will build
you up on your most holy faith AND keep
you in the love of God.** Praying in the spirit
will *keep* you in the God kind of love. It
will keep you in the love walk. If you get
mad at someone, pray in the spirit for an

hour. I don't believe you can come out of your prayer closet and still be mad after praying in the spirit for an hour. Keep yourselves in the love of God. God won't do it for you: you must do it yourself, by praying in the Holy Ghost.

Faith does not fail, for *it is a law.*

Your faith can fail to produce when you fail to walk in love.

Love never fails.

Love will always prevail through faith.

Faith will always prevail through love. (1 Corinthians 13; Galatians 5:6).

PRODUCTION FAILURE

Lack of knowledge will keep your faith from working. Sometimes we have thought that it was God trying us. I have heard many Christians say, "God has taken everything I had because He didn't want me to glory in the things of this earth." No, it is not so. They have been deceived by satan. God didn't do it. My Father didn't do it. He is the giver. He told Israel they would be the head and not the tail, above and not beneath, blessed coming in and going out. When you believe that God did it, and fall for that lie, you become an easy target for satan. He'll take every dime you have and leave you penniless. If he could, he would do it to every believer. ". . . your adversary the devil, as a roaring lion, walketh about, seeking whom he may devour" (1 Peter 5:8). The knowledge of God's Word will keep him from devouring you.

The most devastating blow to your faith is to believe that God is the taker instead of the giver. Not knowing who the troublemaker is will make more trouble for you. A good book to read on this subject is *The Troublemaker* by Kenneth Copeland. I will simply advise you to go to the Bible and begin to draw the battle line. The battle line is John 10:10, "The thief cometh

*Copeland, Kenneth, *The Troublemaker*, published by Kenneth Copeland Publications, P. O. Box 3407, Fort Worth, TX 76105.

not, but for to steal, and to kill, and to destroy: I am come that they might have life, and that they might have it more abundantly."

"Building up yourselves on your most holy faith, praying in the Holy Ghost." Take Paul's advice, and pray in the spirit, building yourself up spiritually. It will keep you in the love of God.

Yes—Faith works, but it can be destroyed by fear, lack of knowledge, envy, strife, and failing to walk in love. There are other things, of course, but these are the major ones. Just because you are a faith man, or a faith woman today, doesn't mean you will be thirty days from now, if you don't do what Peter said to do in 1 Peter 5:8,9: "Be sober, be vigilant; because your adversary the devil, as a roaring lion, walketh about, seeking whom he may devour: Whom resist stedfast in the faith . . . ."

Have you ever wondered why satan is seeking?

Because there are some he can't
devour! If he ever catches your guard
down; walking out of love; in strife and
unforgiveness, you may not be a faith
person the next thirty days.

PRODUCE OR FAIL

Faith comes from the incorruptible
seed: the Word of God.

To ask, "Can faith fail?" is like asking,
"Can a seed fail to produce?" A seed will
fail to produce if not cared for properly. It
will fail to do what it was created to do if it
is not planted in soil that is fertile. It must
be planted at the right time, in the right
place, and protected until it brings forth the
desired results. If you don't plant the seed
properly, it will fail. If you abandon it after
planting, it will fail most of the time. If you
don't protect it from insects, birds, and
other enemies after it comes up, it will fail
to produce the measure it is capable of
producing.

It is not always a matter of the seed failing, but a question of, "Did you cause it to fail?" The seed was designed to produce. **It knows how.** The question is, "Did your action or failure to act cause it to *produce or fail?*"

Charles Capps is a former farmer and land developer who travels throughout the United States, teaching and preaching God's Word. He shares from practical, first-hand experience how Christians can apply the Word to the circumstances of life and live victoriously.

Besides authoring several books, including the best-selling *The Tongue, A Creative Force*, Charles also has a nationwide radio ministry called "Concepts of Faith."

Charles and his wife Peggy make their home in England, Arkansas. Both their daughters, Annette and Beverly, are involved in the ministry.

For a free brochure of books and tapes by Charles Capps, write:

Charles Capps Ministries
Box 69
England, AR 72046

BOOKS BY CHARLES CAPPS

Angels

The Tongue — A Creative Force

Releasing the Ability of God
Through Prayer

Authority in Three Worlds

Changing the Seen
and
Shaping the Unseen

Can Your Faith Fail?

Faith and Confession

God's Creative Power
Will Work for You
(also available in Spanish)

God's Creative Power for Healing

Success Motivation
Through the Word

God's Image of You

Seedtime and Harvest

Hope — A Partner to Faith

How You Can Avoid Tragedy

Kicking Over Sacred Cows

Substance of Things

The Light of Life

Hebrews Syllabus

How To Have Faith In Your Faith

Available at your local bookstore.

Harrison House
P. O. Box 35035 • Tulsa, OK 74153

A BEST-SELLING
CHARLES CAPPS BOOK

WHY TRAGEDY HAPPENS TO CHRISTIANS

How often have you heard the question: "They were such good Christians! Why did this happen to them?" Many believers' lives have been overwhelmed needlessly by defeat and tragedy.

Wrong speaking, wrong praying, and wrong believing will destroy your faith. Praying "If it be Thy will" has opened many doors for the devil's opportunity when God's will is already revealed in His Word.

This book was written to free you and to help you avoid tragedy in your life. Once you taste victory, you will never again have a desire to experience defeat. You can learn to apply the principles of God's wisdom to your life and defeat the devil.

A BEST-SELLING
CHARLES CAPPS BOOK

AUTHORITY IN THREE WORLDS

"The name of Jesus will work, not only in this earth, but that name has authority in three worlds. The Body of Christ stands in a unique position in this dispensation of having authority in all three worlds . . .

"He said that every knee should bow; beings in heaven, beings in the earth, and beings under the earth: including principalities, powers, and rulers of darkness.

"We stand in a unique position through that Name. We can summon the aid of all heaven to work in our behalf . . . ."

A BEST-SELLING
CHARLES CAPPS BOOK

THE TONGUE A CREATIVE FORCE

"Christianity is called the Great Confession, but most Christians who are defeated in life are defeated because they believe and confess the wrong things. They have spoken the words of the enemy. And those words hold them in bondage. Proverbs 6:2 says, **Thou art snared with the words of thy mouth.**

"Words are the most powerful things in the universe . . .

"God created the universe with the spoken WORD . . .

"Spoken words program your spirit (heart) either to success or defeat."

The Harrison House Vision

Proclaiming the truth and the power
Of the Gospel of Jesus Christ
With excellence;

Challenging Christians to
Live victoriously,
Grow spiritually,
Know God intimately